FUNNY V
KNOCK

FOR KIDS

150 VALENTINE'S DAY JOKES FOR CHILDREN

BY
I . P HAPPY

Printed Worldwide
First Printing, 2017

ISBN :1543014542

1. Knock Knock

Who's there?

Howard

Howard who?

Howard you like a big kiss!

2. Knock Knock

Who's there?

Pea's

Pea's who?

Pea's will you be my valentine!

3. Knock Knock

Who's there?

Arthur

Arthur who?

Arthurose chocolates for me?!

4. Knock Knock

Who's there?

Eyesore

Eyesore who?

Eyesore do love you!

5. Knock Knock

Who's there?

Iguana

Iguana who?

Iguana hold your hand!

6. Knock Knock

Who's there?

Orange

Orange who?

Orange you glad I love you!

7. Knock Knock

Who's there?

Olive

Olive who?

Olive you too!

8. Knock Knock

Who's there?

Emma

Emma who?

Emma hoping you'll be my valentine!

9. Knock Knock

Who's there?

Justin

Justin who?

Justin time to be your valentine!

10. Knock Knock

Who's there?

Oscar

Oscar who?

Oscar if she likes me!

11. Knock Knock

Who's there?

Cantaloupe

Cantaloupe who?

Cantaloupe with you tonight?!

12. Knock Knock

Who's there?

Happy

Happy who?

Happy Valentine's Day!

13. Knock Knock

Who's there?

Frank

Frank who?

Frank you for my flowers!

14. Knock Knock

Who's there?

Will

Will who?

Will you be my valentine?!

15. Knock Knock

Who's there?

Halibut

Halibut who?

Halibut a hug!

16. Knock Knock

Who's there?

Value

Value who?

Value be my valentine?!

17. Knock Knock

Who's there?

General Lee

General Lee who?

General Lee I don't blush this much!

18. Knock Knock

Who's there?

Luke

Luke who?

Luke at all your presents!

19. Knock Knock

Who's there?

Anita

Anita who?

Anita give you a kiss!

20. Knock Knock

Who's there?

Mike

Mike who?

Mike I take you to dinner?

21. Knock Knock

Who's there?

Harry

Harry who?

Harry up and give me a hug!

22. Knock Knock

Who's there?

Abbott

Abbott who?

Abbott time you were my valentine!

23. Knock Knock

Who's there?

Pooch

Pooch who?

Pooch your arms around me!

24. Knock Knock

Who's there?

Sherwood

Sherwood who?

Sherwood like to give you a kiss!

25. Knock Knock

Who's there?

Luke

Luke who?

Luke at all your flowers!

26. Knock Knock

Who's there?

Will

Will who?

Will you go to dinner with me?

27. Knock Knock

Who's there?

Pea's

Pea's who?

Pea's can I have a kiss!

28. Knock Knock

Who's there?

Wanda

Wanda who?

Wanda be my valentine?

29. Knock Knock

Who's there?

Carmen

Carmen who?

Carmen, please be my valentine!

30. Knock Knock

Who's there?

Noah

Noah who?

Noah give me a kiss!

31. Knock Knock

Who's there?

Alpaca

Alpaca who?

Alpaca your bags, were going away for valentines!

32. Knock Knock

Who's there?

Hugh

Hugh who?

Hugh should be my valentine!

33. Knock Knock

Who's there?

Annie

Annie who?

Anniebody gonna give me a kiss?!

34. Knock Knock

Who's there?

Witches

Witches who?

Witches the way to your heart?

35. Knock Knock

Who's there?

Leaf

Leaf who?

Leaf me some chocolates!

36. Knock Knock

Who's there?

Urine

Urine who?

Urine love!

37. Knock Knock

Who's there?

Lettuce

Lettuce who?

Lettuce have a kiss!

38. Knock Knock

Who's there?

Honey Bee

Honey Bee who?

Honey Bee my valentine!

39. Knock Knock

Who's there?

Wooden shoe

Wooden shoe who?

Wooden shoe want to be my valentine?

40. Knock Knock

Who's there?

Iva

Iva who?

Iva some flowers for you!

41. Knock Knock

Who's there?

Pauline

Pauline who?

I think I'm Pauline in love with you!

42. Knock Knock

Who's there?

Butch

Butch who?

Butch your arms around me!

43. Knock Knock

Who's there?

Jimmy

Jimmy who?

Jimmy a kiss!

44. Knock Knock

Who's there?

Honeydew

Honeydew who?

Honeydew you know how cute you look right now?

45. Knock Knock

Who's there?

Juno

Juno who?

Juno I love you right?

46. Knock Knock

Who's there?

Aldo

Aldo who?

Aldo anything for you!

47. Knock Knock

Who's there?

Egg

Egg who?

Eggcited to be your valentine!

48. Knock Knock

Who's there?

Candice

Candice who?

Candice be love im feeling right now?

49. Knock Knock

Who's there?

Al

Al who?

Al be your valentine if you open the door!

50. Knock Knock

Who's there?

Juan

Juan who?

You're the Juan for me!

51. Knock Knock

Who's there?

I love

I love who?

Aww, I love who too!

52. Knock Knock

Who's there?

Butter

Butter who?

I Butter be your valentine!

53. Knock Knock

Who's there?

Keith

Keith who?

Keith me! (Kiss)

54. Knock Knock

Who's there?

Iran

Iran who?

Iran to tell you I love you!

55. Knock Knock

Who's there?

Aardvark

Aardvark who?

Aardvark 100 miles to be your valentine!

56. Knock Knock

Who's there?

Lemmy

Lemmy who?

Lemmy give you a kiss!

57. Knock Knock

Who's there?

Ivana

Ivana who?

Iva be yours!

58. Knock Knock

Who's there?

Howie

Howie who?

Howie gonna eat all these chocolates?!

59. Knock Knock

Who's there?

Ice cream

Ice cream who?

Ice cream if you don't let me be your valentine

60. Knock Knock

Who's there?

Annie

Annie who?

Anniebody want to be my valentine? :(

61. Knock Knock

Who's there?

Dozen

Dozen who?

Dozen anyone want to give me a kiss?

62. Knock Knock

Who's there?

Needle

Needle who?

Needle little love on valentine's day!

63. Knock Knock

Who's there?

A herd

A herd who?

Aherd you fancy me?

64. Knock Knock

Who's there?

Noah

Noah who?

Noah anyone who'll be my valentine?

65. Knock Knock

Who's there?

Anita

Anita who?

Anita valentines date!

66. Knock Knock

Who's there?

Annie

Annie who?

I would do Anniething for you!

67. Knock Knock

Who's there?

Cher

Cher who?

Cher would love to be your valentine!

68. Knock Knock

Who's there?

Police

Police who?

Police be my valentine!

69. Knock Knock

Who's there?

Abby

Abby who?

Abby valentines day!

70. Knock Knock

Who's there?

Kenya

Kenya who?

Kenya give me a kiss

71. Knock Knock

Who's there?

Kenya

Kenya who?

Kenya give me a kiss?

72. Knock Knock

Who's there?

Carrie

Carrie who?

Carrie these flowers whilst I hug you!

73. Knock Knock

Who's there?

Shelby

Shelby who?

Shelby my valentine!

74. Knock Knock

Who's there?

Anee

Anee who?

Anee one too love out there

75. Knock Knock

Who's there?

Will

Will who?

Will you hug me?!

76. Knock Knock

Who's there?

Otto

Otto who?

Otto know, I just wanted to say I love you!

77. Knock Knock

Who's there?

Heidi

Heidi who?

Heidi-cided to give me a kiss!

78. Knock Knock

Who's there?

Cash

Cash who?

Im nuts about you!

79. Knock Knock

Who's there?

Saide

Sadie who?

Sadie 3 magic words (i love you)!

80. Knock Knock

Who's there?

Aida

Aida who?

Aida lot of love for you!

81. Knock Knock

Who's there?

Claire

Claire who?

Claire the way, my valentine is coming!

82. Knock Knock

Who's there?

Luke

Luke who?

Luke at how pretty you are :)

85. Knock Knock

Who's there?

Soar

Soar who?

Soar you gonna be my valentine or not?

86. Knock Knock

Who's there?

Roach

Roach who?

Roach you a love letter for valentines day!

87. Knock Knock

Who's there?

Ben

Ben who?

Ben waiting my whole life for someone like you!

88. Knock Knock

Who's there?

Ooze

Ooze who?

Ooze gonna be my valentine?

89. Knock Knock

Who's there?

Marry

Marry who?

Marry me!

90. Knock Knock

Who's there?

Ayew

Ayew who?

Ayew busy on valentines day?

91. Knock Knock

Who's there?

Love

Love who?

I LOVE YOU!

92. Knock Knock

Who's there?

Lenna

Lenna who?

Lenna little closer and give me a kiss

93. Knock Knock

Who's there?

Cute

Cute who?

You

94. Knock Knock

Who's there?

Waddle

Waddle who?

Waddle I do without you?

95. Knock Knock

Who's there?

Pretty

Pretty who?

Pretty you!

96. Knock Knock

Who's there?

Water

Water who?

Water you doing this valentines day?

97. Knock Knock

Who's there?

Kiwi

Kiwi who?

Kiwi have a smooch?

98. Knock Knock

Who's there?

Beef

Beef who?

Beefore you run, I just want to say I love you!

99. Knock Knock

Who's there?

Wooden shoe

Wooden shoe who?

Wooden shoe like a kiss?

100. Knock Knock

Who's there?

Amarill

Amarill who?

Amarilly into you!

101. Knock Knock

Who's there?

Amy

Amy who?

Amy fraid im in love with you!

102. Knock Knock

Who's there?

Ken

Ken who?

Ken we be boyfriend and girlfriend?

103. Knock Knock

Who's there?

Howard

Howard who?

Howard you like to be my valentine?

104. Knock Knock

Who's there?

Pea's

Pea's who?

Pea's be my boyfriend / girlfriend

105. Knock Knock

Who's there?

June

June who?

June-know your my valentine right?

106. Knock Knock

Who's there?

Hugh

Hugh who?

Hugh are the best valentine ever!

107. Knock Knock

Who's there?

Frank

Frank who?

Frank you for being amazing!

108. Knock Knock

Who's there?

Arthur

Arthur who?

Arthurose valentines kisses for me?!

109. Knock Knock

Who's there?

Eyesore

Eyesore who?

Eyesore do want you to be my valentine!

110. Knock Knock

Who's there?

Iguana

Iguana who?

Iguana be yours!

111. Knock Knock

Who's there?

Ivana

Ivana who?

Ivana give you a kiss!

112. Knock Knock

Who's there?

Justin

Justin who?

Justin time to give you a kiss!

113. Knock Knock

Who's there?

Harry

Harry who?

Harry up and kiss me!

114. Knock Knock

Who's there?

Hugh

Hugh who?

Hugh-pid!

115. Knock Knock

Who's there?

Alden

Alden who?

When you're Alden with your dinner, will you

be my valentine?

116. Knock Knock

Who's there?

Avery

Avery who?

Avery nice guy with flowers and choco-lates!

117. Knock Knock

Who's there?

Moustache

Moustache who?

I moustache you for a kiss!

118. Knock Knock

Who's there?

Gwen

Gwen who?

Gwen you gonna give me a hug?

119. Knock Knock

Who's there?

Collie

Collie who?

Collie-flowers and chocolates!

120. Knock Knock

Who's there?

Sofa

Sofa who?

Sofa I haven't had any cards on valentines day :(

121. Knock Knock

Who's there?

Window

Window who?

Window I get hugs and kisses?

122. Knock Knock

Who's there?

Adore

Adore who?

Adore you, who else!

123. Knock Knock

Who's there?

Baby

Baby who?

Baby love, my baby love!

124. Knock Knock

Who's there?

Gray

Gray who?

Gray-z about you!

125. Knock Knock

Who's there?

Halibut

Halibut who?

Halibut a kiss, sweetie?

126. Knock Knock

Who's there?

Hope

Hope who?

Hope you'll be my valentine!

127. Knock Knock

Who's there?

Hymen

Hymen who?

Hymen the mood 4 u!

128. Knock Knock

Who's there?

Ida

Ida who?

Ida know why I love you like I do

129. Knock Knock

Who's there?

Pyjamas

Pyjamas who?

Pyjamas around me and give me a kiss!

130. Knock Knock

Who's there?

Wiccan

Wiccan who?

Wiccan be boyfriend and girlfriend!

131. Knock Knock

Who's there?

Willy

Willy who?

Willy-oo marry me?

132. Knock Knock

Who's there?

York

York who?

York-coming to give me hugs and kisses?

133. Knock Knock

Who's there?

Wendy

Wendy who?

Wendyou want to be my valentine?

134. Knock Knock

Who's there?

Warrior

Warrio who?

Warrior been all my life?

135. Knock Knock

Who's there?

Kante

Kante who?

I Kante stop thinking about you!

136. Knock Knock

Who's there?

Howie

Howie who?

Howie gonna be valentines?!

137. Knock Knock

Who's there?

Al

Al who?

Al give you a kiss if you open the door!

138. Knock Knock

Who's there?

Noah

Noah who?

Noah be my valentine!

139. Knock Knock

Who's there?

Jimmy

Jimmy who?

Jimmy some flowers for valentines day!

140. Knock Knock

Who's there?

Carmen

Carmen who?

Carmen, give me a kiss!

141. Knock Knock

Who's there?

A herd

A herd who?

A herd you want to be my valentine?

142. Knock Knock

Who's there?

Voodoo

Voodoo who?

Voodoo you want to be your valentine?

143. Knock Knock

Who's there?

Stopwatch

Stopwatch who?

Stopwatch you're doing and be my valentine!

144. Knock Knock

Who's there?

Some

Some who?

Some day we'll be each others valentines!

145. Knock Knock

Who's there?

Annie

Annie who?

Annie chance of a kiss?

146. Knock Knock

Who's there?

Pizza

Pizza who?

You've stolen a pizza my heart

147. Knock Knock

Who's there?

Wood

Wood who?

Wood you be mine?

148. Knock Knock

Who's there?

Butter

Butter who?

You're my butter half!

149. Knock Knock

Who's there?

Honey Bee

Honey Bee who?

Honey Bee mine!

150. Knock Knock

Who's there?

Fondu

Fondu who?

Im Fondu YOU!

Made in the USA
Lexington, KY
08 February 2018